Galatians

Redeeming Grace and the Cross of Christ

Sophron Studies
Sound Doctrine…Sound Thinking…Sound Living

Keri Folmar, Series Editor

MELISSA MCPHAIL
LISA MENCHINGER

CruciformPress

© 2020 by Sophron Studies. All Rights Reserved
CruciformPress.com | info@CruciformPress.com

"I know Melissa and Lisa personally and commend them for their love for the word of God and their commitment to equipping women with the truth of Scripture. They are also excellent students and teachers of the Bible. These studies are full of good insight, good wisdom, and good questions. They will serve the church well."
Kevin DeYoung, Senior Pastor, Christ Covenant Church (Matthews, NC), Assistant Professor of Systematic Theology, Reformed Theological Seminary (Charlotte)

"*Galatians: Redeeming Grace and the Cross of Christ* engages the mind and heart of a woman. Its inductive method provides accessible questions and tools that help equip women not only to think biblically about the freedom that Christ offers us in this New Testament epistle, but also the encouragement to live these truths out in the context of community."
Karen Hodge, Coordinator of Women's Ministries for the Presbyterian Church in America, and author of *Life-Giving Leadership* and *Transformed: Life-Taker to Life-Giver*

"This is a great inductive study through the book of Galatians. It takes you deep into Scripture as you explore the transformative power of the gospel in Paul's life and his parental affection for the Galatian church. Paul's ministry reminds us to consider whose approval we are seeking… that of man or God? Through this study you will grow in your understanding of God and his work of justification and sanctification, as well as our adoption into a glorious relationship with him. I commend to you this rich study of the book of Galatians."
Teresa Caldwell, Director of Women's Ministries at Christ Covenant Church (Matthews, NC)

"The stated goal of *Galatians: Redeeming Grace and the Cross of Christ* is to enable the Bible student to understand sound doctrine which leads to sound thinking, inevitably producing sound living. Thus, the authors intend not so much to teach Scripture as to teach how to study Scripture. In so doing, they help the student develop a reasonable method for understanding the meaning of Scripture. The authors encourage students of the Bible to discover that God's Word when rightly understood will infallibly lead to the One who is the Way, the Truth, and the Life. In doing this they echo Isaiah's refrain, 'this is the way, walk ye in it.' (Isaiah 30:21)"
Rev. Michael A. Braun, Th.m.

Welcome!

We're so glad you're starting this study of Galatians! This is an inductive study. If this method is unfamiliar to you, don't worry. This book will provide you with simple directions at every step.

This study is ideal for use in a group setting but can also be helpful for personal Bible study. You will study one portion of Scripture at a time, beginning with the first verse of Paul's letter to the Galatians and continuing to the end. The Sophron Series approach to Bible study ensures proper context, so in the pages that follow you will not merely study Galatians, you will also see how it fits into other key sections of Scripture.

What will you get out of this study? Much of that depends on you. The Bible is first and foremost about God, and he gave us the Bible so we could know him. Therefore, the proper goal of Bible study is not merely to gain more Bible knowledge. Rather, by that knowledge and the empowering of the Holy Spirit, we come to better know God himself!

So think of your participation in this study as triggering a sowing-and-reaping principle. As we sow the Word of God into our hearts and minds, we advance in *sound doctrine*, *sound thinking*, and *sound living*. We reap a greater knowledge and closer experience of God himself, rejoicing in our hope of eternal life (Titus 1:2) and growing in the grace and knowledge of our Lord and Savior Jesus Christ (2 Peter 3:14).

It is our prayer that through this study your roots will begin to grow deep into God's love and his Word. For roots to grow deep, there must be cultivation—the hard work of tilling, sowing, pruning, and watchfulness. Deep spiritual roots take time, effort, and dependence on Almighty God! Be patient and enjoy your time with the Lord as you interact with Jesus Christ, the Word.

We would love to hear from you as you learn to study inductively and come to better know our Lord through Galatians. Visit our website at www.sophronstudies.com and send us an email! Now, enjoy *Galatians: Redeeming Grace and the Cross of Christ*.

– Melissa McPhail and Lisa Menchinger

Melissa McPhail and Lisa Menchinger, longtime members of Christ Covenant Church in Matthews NC, are the founders and authors of the Sophron Series.

Lisa has been a Children's Ministry Director, a Board Member of a Pregnancy Resource Center, and currently serves on the women's leadership team at Christ Covenant. She has been studying Scripture and teaching women for more than 25 years. She and her husband have three young-adult children and a son-in-law.

Melissa is a women's Bible study teacher, mentor, and leader for women's ministries. She is married to John and they have four sons. She has been a stay-at-home mom for 19 years.

This is the first Sophron Study to be published by Cruciform Press.

Galatians: Redeeming Grace and the Cross of Christ

Print / PDF ISBN: 978-1-949253-24-5

Published by Cruciform Press, Minneapolis, Minnesota. Copyright © 2020 by Sophron Studies. All rights reserved. Unless otherwise indicated, all Scripture quotations are taken from: The Holy Bible: English Standard Version, Copyright © 2001 by Crossway Bibles, a division of Good News Publishers. Used by permission. All rights reserved. Italics or bold text within Scripture quotations indicates emphasis added. Scripture quotations marked NLT are taken from the Holy Bible, New Living Translation, copyright © 1996, 2004, 2015 by Tyndale House Foundation. Used by permission of Tyndale House Publishers Inc., Carol Stream, Illinois 60188. All rights reserved.

Contents

Sophron Studies	Introduction	5
Book Survey	Lesson One: **Galatians 1:1 – 6:18**	9
The Gospel of Christ	Lesson Two: **Galatians 1**	15
Paul Preaches Christ	Lesson Three: **Galatians 1:1–10**	21
Called through Grace	Lesson Four: **Galatians 1:11–24**	31
Truth Preserved	Lesson Five: **Galatians 2:1–10**	39
For Purpose	Lesson Six: **Galatians 2:11–21**	51
For It Is Evident	Lesson Seven: **Galatians 3:1–9**	60
It's a Promise	Lesson Eight: **Galatians 3:10–20**	72
If You Belong to Christ	Lesson Nine: **Galatians 3:19-29**	83
Slaves to Sons	Lesson Ten: **Galatians 4:1–11**	94
Gospel Blessedness	Lesson Eleven: **Galatians 4:12–20**	104
Your Mother	Lesson Twelve: **Galatians 4:21–31**	113
Gospel Freedom	Lesson Thirteen: **Galatians 5:1–12**	125
Covenant Community	Lesson Fourteen: **Galatians 5:13–26**	136
Gospel Responsibilities	Lesson Fifteen: **Galatians 6:1–18**	148
Review and Reflection	Lesson Sixteen: **Galatians 1 – 6**	162
Appendix	Guide to Word Studies	172

Delight in the Word

Don't miss these fully inductive Bible studies for women from Keri Folmar!

Endorsed by Kristi Anyabwile, Connie Dever, Gloria Furman, Kathleen Nielson, and Diane Schreiner, the *Delight in the Word* series currently consists of six volumes covering Philippians, James, Ephesians, the Gospel of Mark (two-volume set), and Titus.

bit.ly/DITWstudies

Sophron Studies

Sound Doctrine…Sound Thinking…Sound Living

Sophron Studies is a Reformed, inductive, in-depth approach to the study of God's Word. *Sophron* (pronounced so-frone) is the Greek word for a sound mind. It is curbing one's desires and impulses with self-control and temperance. As believers, we need to be women who study and delight in God and his Word, women who train to have a mind centered on God and renewed by truth (Romans 12:1–2).

A *sophron* mind is God's design for every believer. A *sophron* woman has a wise and sound mind and uses sound judgment; she cultivates prudence and exercises restraint over all her thoughts, whims, plans, passions, and pursuits of desire. A *sophron* woman trains to conform her mind to Jesus Christ: she is single-minded.

A woman who is not *sophron* could indulge impure and irrational thoughts; she may allow her mind to wander without caution. The mindless woman becomes a forgetful hearer (James 1:25), is sluggish in her walk (Hebrews 6:12), and one who moves away from the hope of the gospel of our Lord Jesus Christ (Colossians 1:23).

Who is the *sophron* woman? Who is the woman who is not? If we are not training our thinking to be captivated with our Savior, we end up divided in our thinking, unstable, and fearful. The sober-minded woman can become unrestrained in her mind when she is angered or fearful.

The *sophron* woman and the un-*sophron* woman could indeed be the same woman.

Sophron Studies is designed to encourage you to stay focused on our only hope, Jesus Christ! Make it a habit to set your mind on the things above (Colossians 3:1–2). Study diligently to know him through his Word, to be a woman of a sound *sophron* mind.

The Process of Study

S — Survey

Read prayerfully, with purpose. Read to survey, or gain an overview—to lay the contextual foundation (per the lesson's instruction). There are guided surveys throughout the study to aid your overview.

O — Observation

Observe only the basic facts by looking at specific questions in the lessons. Questions will guide you to consider: What is the context? Who is it about? Why? When did this happen? How?

P — Particulars

Study the details of a given section of Scripture through interpretation by way of cross-references, lists, charts, and defining words in the original Greek or Hebrew language. (The Appendix, "Guide to Word Studies," provides additional guidance.)

H — Harmonization

Begin to better understand the harmony or context of the passage as the author intended. Begin also to connect parts of Scripture to see the Bible as a whole. Context is crucial to understanding!

R — Reiteration

This is an important exercise that requires you to summarize what you have learned. To rewrite, recap, and recount what you have learned—to own the section of Scripture you have studied.

O — Obedience

How does what you have learned affect you? Agree and accept God's Word as truth. How will you apply that truth to your life? How will the biblical author's message enable you to have a higher view of God? Sound doctrine will lead to sound thinking, which will be evidenced in sound living. Obedience is application, and application is obedience.

N — Nourishment

The Word of God is the milk that we are to long for (1 Peter 2:2), and it is solid food for the mature who, because of practice, have their senses trained to discern good and evil (Hebrews 5:14). God's Word nourishes your soul and progressively makes you more like Jesus Christ as you practice his Word.

Before You Begin: How to Use This Book

Throughout the sixteen lessons of *Galatians: Redeeming Grace and the Cross of Christ* there will be instructions directing you to annotate, color-code, and mark the text of Galatians. Therefore, having your own printed copy of Galatians will aid in a more effective study as you respond to and interact with the Word of God.

Please visit www.blueletterbible.org or www.biblegateway.com to print your own copy of the Galatians text (chapters one through six) in the ESV for your personal use. However, if you prefer, you may simply use your Bible and mark as you feel comfortable.

When using this book in a group context, complete each lesson individually, prior to attending your group time. We suggest that your group meet weekly and that there be an appointed facilitator to guide your group as you review together what you have seen in Scripture. The *For Further Study* sections included for some lessons are optional and intended to advance your understanding of the passages just studied.

Recommended Materials

There are many modern-day translations of the Bible. Which one most accurately conveys the true meaning? It's best to choose a more-literal translation rather than one that tends to paraphrase Scripture. We very much prefer, for example, the English Standard Version (ESV) as opposed to paraphrases such as the New Living Translation (NLT) or The Message.

Your study of Galatians will be greatly enhanced by the use of sound, reliable study aids. We strongly encourage you to have the following resources and tools available to you as you work through this book.

Online

- www.blueletterbible.org (extensive Bible-study resources for free)
- *optional* — www.biblestudytools.com
- *optional* — www.biblegateway.com

One or More of These Commentaries on Galatians

- *Galatians For You*, by Timothy Keller
- *The MacArthur New Testament Commentary on Galatians*, by John MacArthur
- *The Message of Galatians*, by John Stott

One or More of These Study Bibles

- *The Reformed Study Bible* (our favorite)
- *ESV Study Bible*
- *MacArthur Study Bible*

Supplemental Books *(optional)*

- Bible atlas
- Bible dictionary
- Interlinear Bible

Marking Tools

Pens or highlighters in six colors (we recommend red, orange, yellow, green, and two shades of blue)

Book Survey

Lesson One: Galatians 1:1 – 6:18

Part One: First Impressions

This week's lesson is about observing the facts written in the letter to the Galatians. This is a *survey* to get an overview of the entire book. Begin with prayer, asking the Holy Spirit to teach you. Read through the six chapters of Galatians (using your own printed copy). Answer the following questions.

1. What are your first impressions?

2. What words are repeated?

3. What are the themes in the book?

4. Who is the author?

5. Who are the recipients?

Part Two: God

Read through Galatians again.

1. What do you learn about God from each chapter?

Chapter One	Chapter Two	Chapter Three

2. Review the chart above. Circle the fact that stands out to you the most.

Chapter Four	Chapter Five	Chapter Six

Part Three: Author

Read through Galatians. Look for information about the author.

1. List brief facts about the author (i.e., where he is, what he is doing, and why) to get a general idea of who wrote to the Galatians.

2. Does the author have pastoral qualities? Which ones do you recognize? Why do they seem important?

Part Four: Recipients

Read Galatians again.

1. What is going on with the Galatians? Where are they? Think about their culture: what are they doing, how are they doing it, and why?

2. What information is told about the churches of Galatia? Do some research on the web or in a Bible resource book for information about the region of Galatia.

Part Five: Purpose

Read through Galatians to discover Paul's purpose(s) for writing. Look for language such *as for this reason, so that, in order to, for, because, therefore, nevertheless, indeed, so.*

1. Why did Paul write this letter?

2. Prayerfully think through the purpose of this letter and the issue of adding to faith in Jesus Christ. Why would anyone feel compelled to add to what he did?

3. Consult a commentary, reading only the introduction to Galatians. Please do not read further than the introduction as we do not want to spoil our study in the days ahead. When was this letter written? What other background information did you find that aids in your understanding of Galatians.

For Further Study
The Galatians Heard the Good News

But now that you have come to know God, or rather to be known by God.
–Galatians 4:9

Read Acts 14:1–28.

1. What did Paul and Barnabas do in the Galatian region?

2. Before Paul went to the Galatian region, he was doing ministry work nearby. Why did Paul and Barnabas leave Iconium?

3. How did God use persecution and resistance to advance the gospel for his glory?

4. What happened at Lystra (Acts 14:8–18)?

5. What did Paul do as he recovered from being stoned nearly to death (Acts 14:20)?

6. What did Paul do in Derbe (Acts 14:21)?

7. How does Paul describe the qualifications for church leadership in Titus 1:6–9?

8. Where did Barnabas and Paul go before they set sail for Antioch of Syria (Acts 14:24–28)?

9. What does Luke conclude about Paul's first missionary journey (Acts 14:16, 27–28)?

10. Is the apostle Paul certain the Galatians clearly heard and understood the gospel?

The Gospel of Christ

Lesson Two: Galatians 1

Part One: Survey

Prayerfully read Galatians chapter one.

1. What words are repeated in chapter one?

2. Read chapter one and mark in red every reference to God (Father, Jesus Christ, Holy Spirit). Fill in the chart with facts about God from this chapter.

Father	Son	Holy Spirit
Father	*Jesus Christ*	
Raised Jesus Christ from the dead	*Was raised from the dead/resurrected. Lord.*	

3. Based on the facts in the chart above, describe God. Who is he?

4. What information does Paul tell us about himself? Note every time Paul is mentioned in chapter one and color-code his name and any reference to his name (pronouns) in light blue. Record below all that he wanted the Galatians to know about him.

5. Note every time the author says *you/your* or any other reference to the recipients (i.e., brothers). Color any reference to the recipients in orange. What information does Paul reveal about the recipients?

6. What information is presented about false teachers in chapter one?

7. What is the main verse that best summarizes this chapter? How would you title chapter one?

Part Two: God

Read Galatians chapter one.

1. What stands out to you about God? What did you learn about God that you did not know before?

2. How does Paul describe Jesus to the recipients of his letter (1:1–5)?

3. Have you ever introduced someone to Jesus Christ in this way? How do we typically present Christ to someone?

4. Why do you think Paul began the letter with Christ's resurrection? Read Acts 2:24.

5. Spend some time meditating on these truths of God. How will you praise him?

Part Three: Author

Read Galatians chapter one.

1. How does Paul identify himself? Why do you think he begins the letter this way?

2. Define *apostle 652*. (This is your first word study! Please note, if these are new to you and it seems challenging at first, see "Guide to Word Studies," at the end of the workbook. Word studies get easier with practice!)

3. How does Paul explain how he became an apostle? How did he *not* become an apostle? How does this compare with Mark 3:14–19?

4. What is significant about Paul being an apostle? If Paul was not recognized as an apostle among the Galatians, what would that indicate about his message?

5. What is Paul preaching? What facts does Paul present to the Galatians about the gospel?

Part Four: Recipients

1. You have read chapter one multiple times now. Are you beginning to understand what was going on with the recipients? Why was Paul challenging them, even rebuking them?

2. What was Paul's sense of urgency in writing this letter? Do you think his concern was for his own reputation?

3. Paul was challenging his readers with the gospel. Why would these believers still need to be confronted with the gospel?

4. Why do you need to be continuously confronted with the gospel?

5. Read Acts 14:1–7. What areas make up the Galatian region?

Part Five: Greeting and Worship

1. Does this letter have the same typical greeting and introduction as Paul's other letters? Choose a few of these introductions to read to see how Galatians compares: Romans 1:1–2, 1 Corinthians 1:1–3, 2 Corinthians 1:1–2, Ephesians 1:1–2, Philippians 1:1–2, Colossians 1:1–2, 1 Thessalonians 1:1–2, and 2 Thessalonians 1:1.

2. What can we conclude about why Paul began the letter to the Galatians this way?

3. You've been studying this letter for two weeks. How do you feel about the foundation built by surveying the facts about the churches in Galatia? What questions come to mind concerning Paul, the Judaizers, or the Galatians?

4. In what way do you relate to the Galatians?

5. We study to know God, ascribing to God his "Worth-ship." Spend time meditating and praying for what God has done and what he is still doing.

Paul Preaches Christ

Lesson Three: Galatians 1:1–10

Part One: Introductions

Read Galatians 1:1–10.

1. Why did Jesus give himself for our sins?

   a. Define *deliver 1807*.

   b. Who is glorified because you were delivered?

2. From what have Christians been delivered? See Matthew 6:13, Colossians 1:13–14, and 1 Thessalonians 1:10.

3. What were the Galatians doing to astonish Paul (cross-reference 4:9–10, 20–21)?

    a. Define *astonish 2296* and *desert 3346*.

4. Does the idea of *turning aside quickly* seem alien to you? Why or why not?

5. Who is troubling the Galatians? What do the troublemakers say about the cross, about Jesus Christ? Read 2:3–5, 3:3, 4:9, 5:7–12, 6:12. Also see Acts 15:5, 2 Corinthians 11:26, and 2 Thessalonians 2:14–16 for information on *those troubled* as well as the troublemakers.

6. What do the troublemakers want to do?

    a. Define *trouble 5015* and *distort 3344*.

7. What would this type of chaos do to any church?

8. What is the warning given in 1:8–9? Why does Paul say the same thing twice?

a. Define *accursed 331*.

9. What is the essence of Paul's twice repeated statements (1:8–9)?

Part Two: Real Dangers

1. The Word of God has no lack of information about and warning against false teachers; it's an urgent subject! Select a couple of the cross-references and see what the authors of Scripture say regarding those who distort the truth: Acts 20:29–32; Romans 16:17–18; 2 Corinthians 11:13–16; Colossians 2:20–23; 1 Timothy 6:3–5; 2 Timothy 3:1–9; Titus 1:9–16; 2 Peter 2:1–3, 18–19; and Jude 4, 8.

2. In what do the false teachers trust?

3. With all that you have learned concerning the urgent danger of distorting the gospel, why is Paul astonished with the Galatians? Why does he say the troublemakers are to be accursed?

Part Three: Grace in Christ

1. Paul describes the gospel as the grace in Christ (1:6). What is the *grace in Christ 5485*?

2. If you had to list the elements of the gospel (his grace) of Jesus Christ, what would you say? Take a moment and jot down the things that come to mind.

3. Paul preaches the grace of Christ, the gospel. Read through chapter one looking for and noting every use of the word *gospel* and color in dark blue. List the information you learn about the gospel below.

4. Cross-reference the following verses and color-code the same way: 2:2, 5, 7; 3:8 and 4:13. What further information do you learn about the gospel?

5. Note what you learn about the gospel from other parts of the New Testament:

    a. Acts 13:23–39

    b. Acts 16:30–33

    c. Romans 1:16–17

d. Romans 10:8–11

   e. Colossians 1:3–6

6. What is the gospel? Define *gospel 2098*.

7. Write a short paragraph explaining the grace of Christ, the gospel.

8. What happens to the gospel if it becomes distorted?

9. How is this threat of false teachers still alive and well in our culture?

10. How will you identify someone who may come and try to pervert the gospel?

11. What safeguards and measures do you take to make sure you do not pass on a distorted gospel?

Part Four: Whom Shall I Please

1. What caused the Galatians to make this astonishing switch (1:1–11)? Who had they decided to please, God or man? Explain your answer.

2. What did Paul contrast in 1:10?

   a. Define *seeking the approval 3982* and *pleased 700*.

3. Imagine if the apostle Paul had been seeking the approval of men. What would he have said differently in 1:1–9?

4. Who are we to seek to please? Why? Note what the following verses teach about seeking to please: Proverbs 29:25; John 5:39–44, 12:42–43; Acts 5:29, 12:1–3; and 1 Thessalonians 2:3–6.

5. What is at the heart of people-pleasing? Whose pleasure do people-pleasers seek, that of God or self?

6. What pleases God the Father? Cross-reference Matthew 3:17 and Hebrews 11:6. What is the implication for us if we are "in Christ"?

7. Are you seeking the approval of man or God? Are you trying to please man? Prayerfully think over these things. These truths are convicting, as well as comforting.

Part Five: Reflect and Confirm

Read through Galatians chapter one again, and then thoroughly and prayerfully review your notes from this week's homework.

1. What have you learned about our Lord and Savior Jesus Christ?

2. How is the Holy Spirit convicting and challenging you?

3. Think about the *present evil age* and all that is going on today. What is

going on around you that causes you to fear? What is going on that makes you thankful for your deliverance?

4. Finish today by reading from various commentary resources. What do biblical scholars say concerning 1:1–10?

For Further Study
The Advance of the Gospel

But you will receive power when the Holy Spirit has come upon you, and you will be my witnesses in Jerusalem and in all Judea and Samaria and to the end of the earth.
—Acts 1:8

Read the following passages of Scripture from the book of Acts, looking at the fulfillment of Jesus' words. Note what you learn about the spread of the gospel. How does Paul's preaching and faithfulness encourage you to remain uncompromising to your witness?

1. The church in Jerusalem and the spread of the gospel in the book of Acts.

   a. Acts 2:41–47

   b. Acts 4:32–33

c. Acts 5:11–14

d. Acts 5:41–42

e. Acts 6:1–8

f. Acts 7:54–60

2. Persecution and spread of the gospel to Judea and Samaria, including Gentiles.

a. Acts 8:1–5

b. Acts 8:25

c. Acts 9:1–3

d. Acts 9:31

e. Acts 10:44–48

f. Acts 11:19–26

3. Modern missionary movement begins—the gospel to the Gentiles.

   a. Acts 13:1–4

   b. Acts 13:48–52

   c. Acts 14:19–28

4. How does the gospel advance in Acts?

5. When did the gospel advance? Was the spread of the gospel in times of peace or in times of turmoil of both?

6. Who, alone, ordains when the door of faith is to be opened?

7. What is the first heresy that began to shake the early church (Acts 15:1)?

8. When did the church grow strong?

9. When will truth and unity be compromised (see Luke 11:14–17)? How does error threaten the church?

10. When the church is attacked, what is the promise and comfort of God (Matthew 16:18)?

Called through Grace

Lesson Four: Galatians 1:11–24

Part One: Paul's Testimony

Prayerfully read Paul's salvation testimony in Galatians 1:11–24 and Acts 9:1–30, 22:3–16. Answer the following questions about Paul's transformation.

1. Describe Paul prior to salvation.

2. How was God's grace shown in Paul's life even before he heard the gospel?

3. What happened to drastically change Paul's life forever?

4. Paul was *called* by God's grace. Define *called 2564*.

5. How did Paul live differently, as a result of his encounter with the Lord? Also, read 2:20.

6. What did others think of Paul's transformation?

7. How was Paul equipped for a life of ministry?

8. Why did Paul share his personal testimony with the Galatians? What facts did he want the Galatians to understand so that they were not easily confused and possibly led astray?

Part Two: Personal Testimony

Read Galatians 1:11–24.

What about you? What has the Author of Life done in your life to bring glory to himself? It is his story, his (holy) calling on your life. Consider the following questions as prompts to begin mapping out God's call on your life, your Jerusalem to Damascus and beyond.

1. What were you like prior to salvation? What was your reputation?

2. How was God's grace shown in your life even before you encountered the gospel?

3. How did you receive the gospel? How did God reveal his Son to you? What happened to drastically and forever change your life?

4. How are you living differently, as a result of Jesus?

5. What did others think of your transformation?

6. How has God equipped you for ministry? See 2 Peter 1:3.

7. Write your personal testimony.

Part Three: Travel Itinerary

Read through Galatians 1:17–24 and note the geographical places Paul references. (Color-code geographical locations in green.)

1. Locate these places on a Study Bible map or Bible atlas, and then sketch Paul's path in the space below. Briefly note what he did in each place and how long he was there (1:17–21).

2. Something is mysterious about the three years of 1:17–18. Read Acts 9:1–26 and answer the following questions.

   a. List everything mentioned about Damascus in Acts 9:1–26.

   b. Why did Paul stay in Damascus for an extended time? Who was with him?

c. Why did Paul leave Damascus (see also 2 Corinthians 11:32–33)?

3. Why did Paul return to Jerusalem (1:18–20)? How was he welcomed? What did Paul do in Jerusalem (1:18–22, Acts 22:17–21)?

4. From Jerusalem, where did Paul go (1:21)? Also, read Acts 9:29–30 and 22:17–21. What new details are presented about Paul's travel to these regions?

5. What was Paul's reputation in Judea (1:22–24)? How did news spread of Paul's transformation? How would this type of news spread today?

6. What point did Paul make by describing his travels to the Galatians?

7. According to Galatians 1, how did God oversee preservation and

protection of his gospel message? How is Paul's work of preserving truth significant to you?

Part Four: Research

Read about Galatians chapter one in your commentary resource(s).

1. Do you understand Paul's tone and plea with the Galatians? Summarize chapter one.

Part Five: Glorifying God

1. How do you see the grace of Christ poured out on the pages of Galatians chapter one?

2. Think about God revealing the gospel to Paul for his glory. Make this a time of worship between you and God.

3. Is the God of the Bible more personal to you now than a few weeks ago? Describe how you know him better through his Word.

4. Chapter one closes by saying "the people were glorifying God because of Paul." Think about your reputation and how you live out the gospel. How does it cause others to glorify God?

5. Describe someone's walk that has caused you to glorify God. Is there

perhaps someone whose life is being persecuted because of his or her faith? Consider sending a note of encouragement to thank someone for his or her faithfulness or to spur one on to endure a trial.

For Further Study
Salvation Transformation

Read Ephesians chapter two.

1. In the chart below, describe the believer. What is she like before Christ? What did God do to change her life? What is she like after Christ?

Before Christ		After Christ
	But God…	

Lesson Four

2. Explain the truth of Ephesians chapter two in Paul's life. What did God do?

Notes on Galatians Chapter 1

Truth Preserved

Lesson Five: Galatians 2:1–10

Part One: Chapter Survey

Read Galatians chapter two.

1. List the repeated words in chapter two.

2. Read chapter two and mark in red every reference to God (Father, Jesus Christ, Holy Spirit). Fill in the chart with facts about God from chapter two.

Father	Son	Holy Spirit

3. Based on the facts in the previous chart, describe God. Who is he?

4. What information does Paul tell us about himself? Note every time *Paul* is mentioned and color-code his name and any reference to his name (pronouns) in light blue. Note all that he wanted the Galatians to know about him.

5. Note every time the author mentions the recipients (you/your); color any reference to the recipients in orange. Note any new information below about the Galatians.

6. Paul is speaking of *another group of people*, but doesn't necessarily name them. What is said about this "party" of people?

7. This chapter brings our attention to five men; you may or may not be familiar with them. On the next two pages, fill in the basic facts about them from chapter two.

Titus	Peter/Cephas

James	John

Barnabas

8. What is the main verse for this chapter? Give this chapter a title.

9. How does chapter one lead into chapter two?

Part Two: Paul's Timeline

Read Galatians 2:1–10.

1. Why did Paul visit Jerusalem this particular time?

2. When does Paul visit Jerusalem?

3. Whom do Paul and Barnabas visit in Jerusalem? Describe the brief visit.

4. Who joined Paul on this Jerusalem trip (2:1–10)? Cross-reference Acts 9:26–30, 12:25, 13:2–3 to find out how they all came together for ministry work.

5. Read Acts 11:22–30, 12:25, and 15:1–31 to gather background information. Summarize Paul's trips to Jerusalem in the chart below.

Galatians 2:1–10	According to Acts 11, 12	According to Acts 15

Lesson Five

6. What questions come to mind regarding the Galatians 2 Jerusalem trip and the timeline? If you could have a few more details from Paul, what would they be?

7. What was the outcome of the meeting, as indicated in 2:1–10? Consult a commentary to get a better understanding of Paul's timeline as it pertains to 2:1–10.

Part Three: Gospel Preservation

Read 2:1–10.

1. Did Paul begin to doubt the original gospel message he had been preaching? What was the issue in which Paul was not about to budge?

2. Did any of the other apostles try to alter Paul's message of the gospel?

3. Read 2:5. Why is this a significant and personal part of history?

4. How had Paul *preserved* the gospel? Define *preserve 1265*.

5. What was the outcome of this Jerusalem visit (2:7–9)? What did this result mean for the Christians back in Antioch?

6. What is your stance on having "zero tolerance" for altering God's gospel?

Part Four: Circumcision

1. With what were Paul and Peter both entrusted (2:7–10)? Explain their gospels.

2. Read chapter two. Mark the word *circumcision* by writing the letter *C* over it. List all that you learn about circumcision in chapter two.

3. Circumcision is also used several times in 5:2–11 and in 6:12–15. Mark *circumcision* in the same way and list what you learn.

4. Why is circumcision a major theme in this letter?

5. What is circumcision? Begin in Genesis 17:9–14, 19–27 and Deuteronomy 10:15–16, 30:6. Then choose a few verses to reference: Luke 2:21; Acts 7:8, 15:5; Romans 2:29, 3:30, 4:11–12, 6:13–15; Philippians 3:3–5; and Colossians 2:11, 3:11. Complete the following chart.

Facts about Circumcision	Physical Circumcision	Spiritual Circumcision

6. What did circumcision represent?

7. Define *circumcision 4059*.

8. Was circumcision necessary for salvation?

9. Why were the false brothers pressing the issue of circumcision?

10. While circumcision is not practiced commonly in churches today, are there similar issues that some churches want to enforce? In what ways do people add to the gospel? What do you feel completes your Christianity?

Part Five: Entrusted with the Gospel

1. Prayerfully read 2:1–10. Of what facts are you certain?

2. Can one be dogmatic about the specific Jerusalem trip Paul refers to? Is the Scripture clear or unclear about these details? Why does Paul give a detailed account of the meeting with *those who seemed influential*?

3. Reflect on the facts and attributes of God described in 2:1–10. Describe him in a personal way.

4. We cannot get far from the topic of people-pleasing and pleasing God. Who are you most influenced by? Whose influence *seems* to dominate in your own life?

5. Consider your spiritual reputation. What gospel do people see that you have been entrusted with? How can others *perceive the grace given to you*?

6. Read from commentary resources concerning 2:1–10.

For Further Study
Who Is Barnabas?

1. What does Paul tell us about Barnabas in Galatians?

2. What do you learn about Barnabas in Acts 4:36–37?

3. How and why did Barnabas initiate a relationship with Saul (Acts 9:26–28)?

4. Read Acts 11:22–30. How had Barnabas showed submission and leadership?

5. How does Luke describe Barnabas in Acts 11:24 and Acts 12:25–13:3?

6. Who set Barnabas apart to work along with Saul (Acts 13:2)?

7. How did Barnabas approach his work for the Lord (Acts 13:42–52; 14:3, 21–28)?

8. What happened that caused Barnabas to part ways with Paul (Acts 15:1–2, 39)?

Lesson Five

9. What is known of the relationship between Barnabas and John Mark (Colossians 4:10)?

10. What were Barnabas's spiritual gifts? How do you see Barnabas, the son of encouragement, displaying his spiritual gifts in Acts 16:36–41?

11. What did Barnabas do for a living (1 Corinthians 9:6)?

12. Based on his actions, how did Barnabas view God?

13. Why would Barnabas be a good friend and ministry partner?

14. With all that you have learned about Barnabas, describe him.

For Purpose

Lesson Six: Galatians 2:11–21

Part One: The Confrontation

Prayerfully read 2:11–21.

1. What is the dramatic event that took place?

2. Why does Paul explain this confrontation to the Galatians?

3. What did Paul observe about Peter's behavior? Define *hypocrisy 5272* and *in step 3716*.

4. What was the reason for the confrontation in 2:13–14?

5. Cross-reference Matthew 23:28, 1 Timothy 4:2, and 1 Peter 2:1. Note what you learn about hypocrisy.

Lesson Six

6. What was significant about Peter's hypocrisy? Describe the likely progression of Peter's sin.

7. Should Peter have known better? Read Acts 10 and Acts 11:1–18.

8. Prior to *certain men* coming from James, do you think Peter had lived out his dietary freedoms (Acts 10)?

9. Who were these *certain men*?

10. Why would James have sent them? Or did he (Acts 15:12–21)?

11. What did Peter really think of Gentiles? Did he remember Jesus' teaching from Mark 7:17–23? Look at Peter's words in Acts 5:29, 10:34–35.

12. Can you relate to Peter's weakness?

Part Two: Just to Be Clear

1. What did Paul and Peter have in common regarding their backgrounds? Their faith? Read 2:11–16 to help you answer.

2. What does Paul say about law, justification, and faith? Read 2:16–21 and mark in a distinct way every time *law*, *justified*, and *faith* are used. List all that you learn in the appropriate column and then complete as directed.

Law	Justified	Faith
What is Paul's point about the law?	What is Paul's point about being justified?	What does Paul proclaim about faith?
Define *law 3551*	Define *justified 1344*	Define *faith 4102*
By the law no one will be_____.	A person is justified by _____. A person is not justified through _____.	What does Paul contrast to faith?

Lesson Six

3. Cross-reference 3:8, 11, 21–26; Romans 3:19–22, 9:30–32; and Titus 3:7. Note what you learn about justification.

4. Define *justification* in your own words.

5. Read again 2:16. What should the Galatians have understood about salvation?

Part Three: Justified

1. Answer the following questions to clarify what Peter was reverting back to.

   a. What was Paul's hypothetical statement to Peter in 2:17?

   b. What is the answer (2:18–20)?

   c. What message is Paul sending to the Galatians by recounting this encounter with Peter?

2. What is Paul's conditional statement in 2:18? What would this statement indicate to Peter?

3. Would Paul want to rebuild anything from his life before salvation in Christ? And if he did, what would he prove? What can the law do for a sinner?

4. What did Paul say about the law from a personal standpoint (2:19–20)?

5. How does Paul give clarity to this in Colossians 2:13–15, 3:9–10? What is the difference in the *old self and the new self*? How does this support 2:19?

6. What is Peter's warning regarding false teachers (see 2 Peter 2:19)?

7. Read 5:1–7. In what ways were the Galatians struggling?

8. How are you like the Galatians? With what do you struggle? To what are you enslaved?

9. What is the good news of Jesus Christ that Paul was preaching and preserving? Why did Christ die for Paul? Why did Christ die for you?

10. Paul's first death is always fresh on his mind (2:19–20). Have you died to the law so that you may live to God? If so, do you ever find yourself

Lesson Six

grieving over the life you died to? Do you attempt to rebuild your past ways (before salvation), even though you fully understand the gospel? What about your old life would you care to rebuild as if Christ were pointless? Are you following Paul's logic of his old ways and the new way (2:19–20)?

Part Four: Living for God

1. How does Paul identify himself with Christ (2:20)? Why?

2. What does it mean that Paul has been *crucified* with Christ? Define *crucify 4957*. Cross-reference Romans 6:6, 2 Corinthians 5:17, and Philippians 1:21.

3. Use a study Bible or a Bible dictionary and research the former practice of *crucifixion*. Summarize it.

4. Knowing what you know about crucifixion, will you boldly identify yourself with Christ?

5. What did Paul tell the Galatians about God's grace (2:21)? Why?

6. Define *nullify 114*.

7. Write out the last five words of chapter two. What thoughts come to mind about Christ's sacrifice? Was it with purpose?

8. Our flesh's natural default begs to be justified by our own works. How are you tempted to exchange God's grace for your works?

9. Summarize and personalize 2:16–21.

10. Do you live like you depend on God's (perfect and past) sacrifice, that it was with purpose? Do you understand the mindset of the Galatian

Lesson Six

believers? Have you come to terms with the freedom he has provided through faith?

Part Five: The Message of Grace

1. Why did the false teachers insist on circumcision and clean eating to be in a right standing with God?

2. The Judaizers followed traditions, rules, and observances. We, too, have unwritten lists of traditions, rules, and observances of "what it takes to be a good Christian." Take a moment to reflect on your list. In your mind, what should a Christian do? In your opinion, what should a Christian never do? What can these lists lead us to think?

3. Spend time meditating on Jesus. What attributes come to mind from Galatians 2?

4. Summarize chapter two, noting what Paul defended and why.

5. Follow up with commentaries through chapter two. Record notes as needed. If time permits, consider listening to a sermon on Galatians.

Notes on Galatians Chapter 2

For It Is Evident

Lesson Seven: Galatians 3:1–9

Part One: Chapter Survey

Prayerfully read Galatians chapter three.

1. How does Paul introduce chapter three?

2. What words or phrases are most repeated in chapter three?

3. Read chapter three. Mark in red every reference to God (Father, Jesus Christ, Holy Spirit). Fill in the chart with facts about God from this chapter.

Father	Son	Holy Spirit

4. Based on the facts in the chart above, describe God. Who is he?

5. What information does Paul tell us about himself? Note every time *Paul* is mentioned and color-code his name and any reference to his name (pronouns) in light blue. Note all that he wanted the Galatians to know about him.

6. Note every time the author mentions the recipients of his epistle, and color with orange. What new information is given about the Galatians?

7. What additional information is given about the false teachers?

8. List the questions Paul asked the Galatians in chapter three.

9. What is the main verse for this chapter? Give this chapter a title.

Lesson Seven

Part Two: Bewitched

Read Galatians 3:1–9.

1. What does Paul call the Galatians? *Define foolish 453*.

2. Describe Paul's tone and rebuke. Why is Paul harsh with the Galatians?

3. What does Paul ask the Galatians in 3:1? Define *bewitched 940*.

4. How did the Galatians see Christ *publicly portrayed* as crucified? Had they really seen Christ crucified with their own eyes? What does this mean?

5. What was Paul's concern for the Galatians? What did they have difficulty believing? How were they to continue to live out their salvation (3:3)?

6. What did the Galatian believers receive? How were they to continue their salvation?

7. How is it that Jesus Christ and his gospel can *perfect* a believer?

   a. Define *perfect 2005*.

   b. What does this tell us about the work of our Savior?

   c. Who is in charge of your sanctification?

8. What did Paul recall to the believers (3:4)? Why is this important to remember?

9. Define *suffer 3958*. How does this help you better understand Paul's reference to the Galatians' suffering (3:4)?

Lesson Seven

10. What happened to cause the Galatians to veer off to wrong thinking? Can you think of a time you veered off to wrong thinking? What was the result?

Part Three: Spirit Living

1. What question did Paul ask the Galatians in 3:5? Define *supplies 2023*.

2. What truth does Paul provide about the Holy Spirit (3:5)?

3. What is Paul contrasting? Why (3:5)?

4. What did the Galatians know about the Holy Spirit as presented in Galatians? Read through 2:19–21, 3:2–3, 5, 14, 5:16–26, 6:8, and 12–13, and mark the word *Spirit* in red. List all that you learned from noting the word *Spirit*.

5. Read through the same passages again (2:20–21; 3:2–3, 5, 14; 5:16–26; 6:8; 12–13) and mark the word *flesh* in brown. List all that Paul says about the *flesh*.

6. Were the Galatians confused about how the Holy Spirit was supplied to them?

7. What did Paul want the Galatians to understand about the Holy Spirit? Is there evidence that supports them having the Holy Spirit?

8. How do you live out your faith? How do you settle the tension between grace and works within your mind?

9. What might a Galatian woman have thought as she heard this truth (3:1–5)? Would she have been pierced with the truth and turned her *bewitched* eyes back to the vividness of the gospel?

Lesson Seven

Part Four: Who Is Father Abraham?

1. Read 3:6–9. With whom does Paul compare the Galatians' faith? What is he emphasizing?

2. Read 3:6–29. Mark in yellow every reference to Abraham and then list all that you learn about Abraham in this section.

3. Who was Abraham? Do a brief character study on Abraham by reading Genesis 11:26–17:27, Romans 4:3–25, and Hebrews 11:8.

4. How is Abraham described in 2 Chronicles 20:7, Isaiah 41:8, and James 2:23?

5. How was Abraham declared righteous (justified) before God (3:6)? How did he believe?

6. Who were the sons of Abraham? Are you a son (daughter) of Abraham? Explain your answer.

7. What did the Scripture do in regard to Abraham's faith (3:8)?

8. What promise would come through Abraham? Why was this promise so important?

9. What was Abraham's part of the contract or agreement?

10. What did Abraham learn of God's grace?

Part Five: We Are of Faith

Prayerfully read Galatians 3:1–9.

1. Are you tempted to condemn the Galatian believers for neglecting Christ and his gospel? Is there anything about the gospel that you struggle

to believe? Are you potentially relying on the works of the law, or are you living out your walk in faith?

2. What should the Galatians vividly continue to keep in mind?

3. What should you vividly keep in mind? How does remembering the gospel daily affect you?

4. Can you live out your sanctification to the end by the flesh and by the Spirit simultaneously (3:3)? Explain your answer.

5. Describe God as portrayed in 3:1–9.

6. How can we hold firm to our Lord and his gospel of grace? Cross-ref-

erence Hebrews 12:1–3 and Philippians 1:6. How does this help you understand 3:1–5?

7. How does Paul's reference to Father Abraham support all that he has been defending?

8. Read commentary resources through 3:9 and summarize 3:1–9.

For Further Study
Where's Your Gaze?

The NLT version renders Galatians 3:1, "Oh, foolish Galatians! Who has cast an evil spell on you? For the meaning of Jesus Christ's death was made as clear to you as if you had seen a picture of his death on the cross."

1. The Galatians had not witnessed the crucifixion, but what had been made clear to them (3:1)?

2. How does the crucifixion affect us? Read 2:19–21.

3. If we have been charmed, mesmerized, or distracted by something other than Christ and his finished work on the cross, what are we (3:1)?

4. Satan is the one behind the *bewitching* or *casting evil spells* on the Galatians (and us). How does he use the *eyes* as a strategic way to entice, tempt, and lure us into sinful desires? Cross-reference 1 John 2:15–17.

5. Satan is a master at making lies appear to be truth and at seducing us to turn our eyes to worthless things rather than the cross. He is the originator of the old "bait and switch"! Read Genesis 3:1–7 and answer the following questions:

   a. Where did it all begin?

   b. Whom did the serpent seek out?

   c. How does he communicate God's Word? Compare Genesis 2:16–17.

   d. What was the goal of his lying and distorting God's Word?

e. How did Eve allow herself to be enticed?

f. How is she like the Galatians?

g. How did her "eyes" play into this (Genesis 3:6)?

h. Did her sin affect just herself? What does she do (Genesis 3:6)?

i. What did Adam do?

j. What was the result of their sin (Genesis 3:7)?

6. Read Psalm 101:3, Matthew 5:27–30, and 2 Corinthians 11:3.

7. We live in a culture of continuous messages, information, lies, enticements, and "bait and switches" that seek to lure us away from Christ. What is the *only* cure? Remember Hebrews 12:1–2. What are we to do?

8. Ask the Lord to show you the areas of weakness and the idols of your heart that tempt you to be enticed by worthless things. Repent and ask for forgiveness. Pray to God to rescue you from the lies, seductions, and condemnations of Satan. Fix your eyes on Jesus Christ!

It's a Promise

Lesson Eight: Galatians 3:10–20

Part One: Law and Faith

1. Read chapter three. Look for and distinctively mark the words *law* and *faith*. List the facts in the chart.

Law	Faith

2. Read over the lists in each category. Sum up the law.

3. What does it mean to rely on the works of the law (3:10)? On what were the Galatians relying?

4. Take a moment to consider something on which you are prone to rely, in order to maintain favor with God.

5. Why would anyone desire to live by or rely on the works of the law? Review 2:16–21.

6. The word *curse* is repeated five times in 3:10–13. Mark this word in a distinct way, and then list what is said about curse.

7. Based on the facts above, what was the curse?

Lesson Eight

a. Define *curse 2671*.

8. Is anyone not guilty before God? Cross-reference Isaiah 53:6 and Romans 3:23–24.

9. What is Paul's point in 3:10?

   a. Who was cursed?

   b. In what kind of spiritual position are the accursed ones?

Part Two: It Is Evident

1. What should be evident to the foolish Galatians (3:11)? Remember Paul's question to the Galatians in 3:2.

2. Were the Galatians living by faith? Define *evident 1212*.

3. How will the righteous live? Cross-reference Romans 1:16–17 and Habakkuk 2:4.

4. What does Paul say to further clarify his point? How does the law operate differently from faith (3:10–12)?

5. How does Paul remind the Galatians of hope? What does he say about redemption (3:13–14)?

6. Define *redeemed 1805*. Cross-reference 4:5, Matthew 20:28, Titus 2:14, and 1 Peter 1:18–19.

7. What does it mean to be *hanged on a tree* (read Deuteronomy 21:18–23, 27:15–26)? Why did Jesus hang on a tree (Acts 5:30, 1 Peter 2:24)?

Lesson Eight

8. Use a study Bible or a biblical website such as www.preceptaustin to research the punishment of being *hanged on a tree*.

9. Should you and I be cursed and hanged on a tree? Instead of suffering from the law's curse, what are we to *receive* (3:14)?

10. How did the Jews feel about a Savior who was hanged on a tree? Why do you think Paul presented the fact that Jesus, our Redeemer, was hanged for our sake? How would this help the Galatians better understand salvation by faith (alone)?

Part Three: The Blessing of Father Abraham

1. Read 3:14–20. What is Paul's argument in this chapter? What did Paul want the Galatians to understand?

2. Why did Christ redeem us from the curse of the law (3:13–14)?

3. How did Paul support his reasoning for receiving the *blessing and the promise* (3:15)?

a. What is the synonym to *promise* in this verse?

b. Define *covenant 1242*.

4. What did Paul want the Galatians to understand about the promise? Read 3:14–29 and mark the word *promise* with a pink star. List all that you learn from marking *promise*. Cross-reference Acts 3:25 and Romans 9:8.

5. In your own words, describe the promise and those affected by it.

a. Define *promise 1860*.

6. How did God make a covenant with Abraham? Read Genesis 15:8–18.

7. What was the sign of the covenant (Genesis 17:10–11)? What was the evidence of promise? See also Romans 15:8.

Lesson Eight

8. What was Paul's argument in 3:17–18? How does this explain the inheritance?

9. What thoughts come to mind about your inheritance and the price paid for it? How can you praise God for his promise?

Part Four: The Law's Purpose

1. One's inheritance does not come by the law. Why then did God give the law (3:18–19)? Cross-reference 3:23–24 and Romans 3:19–20, 4:15, 7:7–25.

2. How long was the law to be in place (3:17–19)? What does *until* imply?

3. How does Paul explain the Offspring (3:16–19)?

4. How was the law put into place (3:19)? How does the New Testament

give further information on this (Acts 7:53, Hebrews 2:2)?

5. What does *intermediary* imply (3:20)? Define *intermediary 3316*.

6. Who was involved as an intermediary when the law was enacted (Deuteronomy 5:5; Exodus 19:9–11, 24:3–8; Acts 7:52–53; Hebrews 2:2)? Why is this significant?

7. Was there a mediator involved in the Abrahamic (faith) covenant (remember Genesis 15)? What does this mean?

8. Who served as a mediator in the new covenant? Cross-reference 1 Timothy 2:5 and Hebrews 8:6, 9:15, 12:24.

9. What does 3:19–20 tell us about God and his promises?

Lesson Eight

10. How is the promise superior to the law? Why was this important for the Galatians to understand?

Part Five: Praise God for His Promise

1. Describe what life would be like under the law, apart from the promise.

2. Can a woman be in a right standing and right relationship with God through the law? Cross-reference Romans 3:23–25 and 6:23.

3. Based on what you have studied in chapter three, how can the curse of the law be removed from a woman? What was Paul proving to the foolish Galatians?

4. Why did the Judaizers need to hold on to the law to prove their religious position? Why was it challenging for the Galatians to understand grace through faith? What were the false teachers urging the Galatians to believe?

5. How did mentioning Abraham help the Galatians *get back to their senses*? Or did they *get back to their senses*?

6. How do you fit into Abraham's story, the story of the covenant of faith?

7. Consult commentary resources through 3:20 and summarize 3:10–20.

8. Spend time meditating on the character of the God who makes an everlasting covenant with us!

For Further Study
The Righteous Shall Live by Faith

How well do you understand the covenants?

1. Complete the chart below, adding information from Galatians 3 to each column as appropriate, then cross-reference the indicated passages. Write how each covenant reveals or points to Christ.

Lesson Eight

The Abrahamic Covenant	The Law of the Covenant
(Genesis 15, Romans 4:5)	(Exodus 19:4–12, 24:3–8, 20:1–21)

The New Covenant of Christ
(Jeremiah 31:31–34, Ezekiel 36:26–27, 2 Corinthians 3:3–18, Hebrews 9:15, 10:15–22)

2. Do all these covenants involve faith? How are they alike? How do they differ?

If You Belong to Christ

Lesson Nine: Galatians 3:19–29

Part One: Why the Law?

1. There are four repeated words in 3:15–29. Mark each of the repeated words in a distinct way, then list everything you learn there about each.

Covenant	Promise

Law	Faith

2. Which came first, the promise or the law? Did the law make the promise void?

3. Who gave the law? Who gave the promise?

4. Read 3:19–29 and Romans 3:19–20, 4:13–15. Why the law? Is the law bad?

5. What does Paul say about sin and transgressions (3:19–22)? How does the law make one aware of sin? Cross-reference Romans 7:5–13.

6. How was the law fulfilled? Cross-reference Matthew 5:17–18 and Romans 8:3–4, 10:4.

7. How has the law revealed your need for God's grace?

8. Read Romans 2:15–29. How does this passage help us to understand the law?

Part Two: Intermediary

1. How was the law put in place (3:19–20)? Why was it necessary for the law to have an intermediary?

2. Is the law contrary to the promises of God (3:21, 2:21)? How is the law different from the promise?

3. What is Paul contrasting in 3:22?

   a. Define *imprisoned 4788*.

4. What was imprisoned (3:22)? Why?

Lesson Nine

5. Who is held captive? Why? Define *held captive 5432*.

6. How long is the captivity (3:23)? Define *revealed 601*.

7. What is the opposite of being held captive (see 5:1)?

8. What message is Paul sending to the Galatians?

Part Three: Guardian

1. Read 3:24–29. What was the law's primary function? Why?

   a. Define *guardian 3807*.

2. Explain how the law is used as a *guardian* to bring one to salvation.

3. How were the Judaizers misunderstanding the law as their guardian?

4. How has the law served its purpose in you? How has the law enabled you to know the Savior, the One who saved you from the penalty and condemnation of the law?

5. Read Ephesians 2:11–20. How does this support what you have learned in Galatians?

6. Read commentary resources on 3:19–25 and summarize the passage.

Part Four: Family

1. Prayerfully read 3:26–29. Who is a *son* of God? How?

2. When does one come to be called a *son of God*? What would the

Gentile Galatians have thought of this? How do you think the Judaizers in Galatia reacted to Paul calling the believers *sons of God*?

    a. Define *son 5207*.

3. Cross-reference John 1:12–13 and Romans 8:14–17. How does Paul explain a believer's identity and unity in Christ (3:27–29)?

4. What does it mean to be baptized into Christ (3:27)? Read Romans 6:3–6 to better understand being *baptized into Christ*.

5. How and when does one *put on Christ*? Cross-reference Romans 13:14, Ephesians 4:21–25, and Colossians 3:9–14.

6. Describe the family God had in mind for himself (3:28–29). How did

he make a blended, dysfunctional, terribly flawed and sinful family work? What is it like to belong to God's family (see 1 Peter 1:3–5)?

7. What does Paul tell the Galatians about their inheritance (3:18, 4:7)? How does sinful man gain an inheritance among the heirs of the Almighty (Titus 2:14)?

8. What is Paul's conclusion in chapter three? Read Ephesians 4:1–6.

Part Five: Summary

1. Review Lessons Seven to Nine. Write a summary of 3:1–29.

2. Why was Abraham the perfect example for Paul to use?

Lesson Nine

3. With all that you have learned concerning the true sons of God, describe yourself as a son (a daughter) of God.

4. Why is Paul upset with the Galatians?

5. Now that you have a better understanding of Paul's purpose in writing, describe the false gospel they were quickly turning to. What gospel were they deserting?

6. Can you personally answer Paul's question in 3:2, "Did you receive the Spirit by works of the law or by hearing with faith?"

7. Read from commentary resources through 3:1–29, and complete the following quiz. Answer each blank with *law* or *promise*.

    a. The _____ was first made to Abraham and to his offspring (Christ).

    b. The _____ came first.

    c. The _____ came four hundred thirty years after the _____ and was added because of transgressions.

d. The inheritance (of faith) comes by _____. It does not come by the _____.

e. The _____ was put in place through angels by an intermediary.

f. The _____ cannot (ever) give life.

g. Righteousness is never through the _____.

h. The _____ held us prisoners until faith came.

i. The _____ was our guardian until Christ came.

j. We are heirs, according to the _____.

For Further Study
Union with Christ

As you have received Christ Jesus the Lord, so walk in him, rooted and built up in him and established in the faith, just as you were taught, abounding in thanksgiving.
–Colossians 2:6-7

1. Organize yourselves into three groups. Assign Galatians chapters one, two, and three, one chapter per group.

2. Working in your assigned group, sort through your assigned chapter to complete the columns below.

3. Present your chapter findings to the class per group.

Because I belong to Christ, I am...	Because I belong to Christ, I am no longer...

Notes on Galatians Chapter 3

Lesson Nine

Slaves to Sons

Lesson Ten: Galatians 4:1–11

Part One: Chapter Survey

Prayerfully read Galatians chapter four.

1. What words are repeated throughout the chapter?

2. Mark in red every reference to God (Father, Jesus Christ, Holy Spirit). Fill in the chart with facts about God from this chapter.

Father	Son	Holy Spirit

3. Based on the facts in the chart above, describe God. Who is he?

4. What information does Paul tell us about himself in chapter four? Note every time *Paul* appears and color-code his name and any reference to his name (pronouns) in light blue. Note all that he wanted the Galatians to know about him.

5. Note every time the author mentions the letter's recipients (*you* or *your*), and color any reference to the recipients in orange. What do you learn about the Galatians?

6. What additional information is given about the false teachers?

7. What is the main verse for this chapter? Give this chapter a title.

8. What is Paul's flow of thought from 3:23–4:11?

Lesson Ten

Part Two: Redeemed under the Law

1. What is the difference between a slave and a son? Complete the chart using 3:22–4:10.

Characteristics of a Slave	Characteristics of a Son

2. Describe the roles and functions of *guardians* and *managers* (4:2). What is the difference between these roles? Define *guardians 2012* and *managers 3623*.

3. When one is under the law's guardian, to what is he or she *enslaved*? Define *enslaved 1402*.

4. What are the *elementary principles of the world*? Cross-reference Leviticus 23:5, 16, 28, 25:4 and Colossians 2:16–23.

5. What do you learn about a son in 4:1–2?

6. How does Paul compare believers/sons with slavery (4:3–5)? When is God's son free from enslavement to the law? How?

7. What did God do at just the right time (4:4)? Why?

8. Review *redeemed* (Lesson Eight, Part Two) and then see 1:4 and 3:13. Summarize what Paul meant by telling the Galatians that Christ came to redeem.

9. What do the following verses teach about redemption?

   a. Mark 10:45

Lesson Ten 97

    b. Ephesians 1:7–10

    c. Colossians 1:13–14

    d. Hebrews 2:14–15

10. What did you do to cause God to send forth his Son, to redeem *you*? Is it sobering for you to consider your unworthiness before your adoption into the family of God? Praise God for adopting his children into his family!

Part Three: Adoption

1. How does one become a daughter of God's family (3:29–4:7)?

2. Who gave you the right to become God's child? Cross-reference John 1:12–13 and 1 John 3:1–2.

3. How has your adoptive Father shown you love?

4. What does one receive as a result of redemption? Define *adoption 5206*.

5. What does the Holy Spirit cry out (4:6)?

6. What did Jesus say in Mark 14:36?

7. Who can utter these words?

8. Define *Abba 5* and *Father 3962*.

9. Consider the privilege of crying out "Abba! Father!" What does your heart say? Does this truth change how you approach God? Did the Galatians understand this? Did the Jews understand this?

10. How did you receive the Spirit? Read Romans 8:14–25 and compare with 4:6–7. Note what you learn about adoption from these passages.

11. What is Paul's conclusion in 4:7? Write out this truth in first person.

12. Note the Trinity's work in your salvation, from slavery to sonship.

13. Are you a daughter? You'll know by the cry of your heart! See the reminders of his love in Romans 5:1–8 and John 3:16. Spend time meditating on your personal redemption and adoption.

Part Four: Heirs through God

1. Read 4:8–11. What was the imminent danger the Galatians were facing?

2. How were they responding to this danger?

3. To what were the Galatians previously enslaved (4:8)? Define *enslaved* *1398*.

4. Cross-reference Ephesians 2:1–3, 11–12. What were we all like formerly, when we did not know God?

5. Remember the gospel is a rescue! Why would the Galatians prefer to have no hope and be without God?

6. What does Paul contrast in 4:9? How is *now* different from before?

7. How did you come to know God? How is it that the God of the Universe can know you? Do you think this statement startled the foolish Galatians into a sober mind?

8. How foolish does it sound to say, "You have made me your daughter. You have adopted me into your family, but I prefer to be a slave"? Summarize the folly of the Galatians.

9. What did Paul fear for the Galatians (4:11–16)?

10. Praise God for his perfect patience! Read 1 Timothy 1:16 and rejoice in our great Lord!

Part Five: Do Not Turn Back

1. Legalism, works, performance—what is your default? What do you tend to go back to that is weak and worthless yet makes you feel like a better Christian? Could this be similar to what Paul was addressing with the Galatians?

2. Review 1:1–10. Had Paul's gospel changed? Has Christ changed? Has the message ever changed? Who changes? What does this tell us about God?

3. Read again 4:1–11. What have you learned about God? Can we ever spend enough time thanking God for purchasing, rescuing, adopting, freeing, and sending his Son to atone for us? Pray that you would not change or shift, that you would not turn back to serving worthless and weak things.

4. Is there a particular way that you have identified with the Galatians?

5. Read commentaries on 4:1–11 and summarize the passage.

Gospel Blessedness

Lesson Eleven: Galatians 4:12–20

Part One: Become as I Am

Prayerfully read chapter four.

1. What was Paul's appeal in 4:1–11? Why is he rebuking his readers?

2. Recall what life was like for the Galatians prior to hearing the good news. To what were they enslaved? What happened that changed their lives?

3. How does Paul address the Galatians in 4:12? What does this tell us about his care for them?

4. What was Paul's desire for the Galatians (4:12)? Cross-reference 1 Corinthians 9:20–22.

5. What was Paul willing to do to for the sake of the gospel?

6. Do you think that Paul may have been arrogant? Read 1 Corinthians 11:1 and 1 Thessalonians 1:6–7. Why does he exhort the Galatians, Corinthians, and the Thessalonians to become like him?

7. What had Paul first preached to the Galatians (4:13)? Why?

8. How do you see God's sovereignty in thwarting Paul's plans so that he preached the gospel to the Galatians?

9. Has there been a time that God thwarted your plans to serve a bigger purpose?

Lesson Eleven

10. Describe the early days of Paul church-planting in Galatia (4:12–15).

Part Two: Received as an Angel of God

1. How had the Galatians received Paul (4:12–15)?

2. Read 1 Corinthians 2:1–5. How had Paul preached the gospel to the Corinthians? What was most significant in what he said (see Romans 10:17)?

3. What did Paul want all believers' faith and conversion to rest in?

4. What do we know to be true about Paul's health condition (4:14)? What is vague or uncertain? Read in a study Bible or Bible dictionary to find out what bodily ailment Paul may have had.

5. Though Paul's condition was a trial to the Galatians, how did they *not* respond? Define *scorn 1848* and *despise 1609*.

6. How had the Galatians changed (4:13–16)? What had become of their blessedness? Define *blessedness 3108*.

7. What must you know to understand *blessedness* (Romans 4:6–8)? How can a believer maintain her blessedness?

8. Do you still count yourself as happy and blessed as when you first heard the good news of the gospel? Are you still receiving the Word with joy? Are you in any danger? Prayerfully think over spiritual decline—it is a process, a slow fade.

9. What is the danger of rejecting what God has said? Read Mark 7:6–13 and 1 Thessalonians 4:7–8.

10. Summarize Paul's affection for the Galatians.

Part Three: Protection

1. What is the shift in the Galatians' devotion and affection for Paul (4:16)? Why the change?

2. Was Paul preaching something to the Galatians now, which they had not heard before? Of what truth had Paul been reminding them?

3. Who or what changed? Is change bad? How does gospel change happen? What happened to cause the Galatians to change (review 1:6–10, 3:1)?

4. What are we to never change? Cross-reference Deuteronomy 4:1–2, Proverbs 30:5–6, and Revelation 22:18–19. What occurs as a result of altering God's Word?

5. How do we hold fast to the Word and guard against distorting it? Cross-reference Psalm 119:1–8, Colossians 1:21–23, Titus 1:9, and Hebrews 10:19–25.

6. What about you? What informs your conscience if it is not the Word of God? Do you think that you would *never* change?

7. Implore the Lord to show you any areas in your life in which you are beginning to shift, change, or distort the gospel of Jesus Christ. Repent and return to the Source of your blessedness.

Part Four: Christ Formed in You

1. What is Paul's observation of the false teachers' relationship to the Galatians (4:17–18)?

2. Read Psalm 5:9–12. How did David describe his enemies? How did David's description of false teachers compare with the Galatians' false teachers?

3. How does God take care of his own (Psalm 5:11–12)?

4. How did Paul refer to the Galatians in 4:19? What metaphor did Paul use in describing his relationship with them in 4:19–20?

5. How do you see the same type of affection in 1 Thessalonians 1:2–3, 2:7–8, and Hebrews 13:17?

6. Paul labored as in the anguish of childbirth to see Christ formed in the Galatians. What did the false teachers selfishly and greedily want to see formed in them?

7. What or who does Paul desire to see formed in the Galatian believers? Define *formed 3445*.

8. Cross-reference Philippians 1:6 and Ephesians 4:11–16. What do you learn about spiritual maturity?

9. Summarize what it means to have Christ formed in you.

10. Had you ever thought about Paul's work in terms of the *anguish of childbirth*? Is there someone who labored over you until Christ was formed in you? Spend time in prayer today thanking God for the faithful men and women who labored over you.

Part Five: Remember and Repent

1. What is Paul's desire in 4:20? Has the tone of the letter changed?

2. Paul is speaking as a parent, like a mom. Why is he perplexed? Define *perplexed 639*.

3. Have you ever been perplexed over someone's walk with God? Has anyone ever been perplexed by your walk?

4. Read 2 Peter 1:3–13. Summarize a believer's responsibility for maturing in her faith.

5. Cross-reference 2 Thessalonians 1:3. Why can Paul *not* say this to the Galatians? Can your pastors and elders pray this passage with sincerity?

6. Do you think Paul labored over the Galatians in vain (4:11)?

7. Read from commentaries on 4:1–20 and summarize the passage.

Your Mother

Lesson Twelve: Galatians 4:21–31

Part One: Father Abraham

1. Cross-reference Romans 7:7 and 12. What facts does Paul present about the law?

2. Remember that Paul was perplexed with the Galatians. What does he ask in 4:21?

3. Do you think you could be led back to the law's bondage? Why would any godly man or woman fall for the law's bondage again (2:11–13)?

4. What might this look like today? Have you been guilty of judging others based on your *own* standards, personal convictions, or rules?

5. How is the Father pleased with you? Read Matthew 3:17, Galatians 2:20, and Colossians 1:27.

6. Who does Paul reintroduce in 4:22? Review 3:6–9 and 14–18.

7. Why did the Jews have a high regard for Abraham?

8. The Pharisees and Sadducees had a high regard for Abraham, too. What did John the Baptist tell them in Matthew 3:7–10? On what were they relying?

9. Who were the Pharisees and Sadducees? Use a study Bible or Bible dictionary to research these groups. (See the Recommended Materials section at the beginning.)

Part Two: Set Free

1. What did Jesus say to the unbelieving Jews in John 8:31–59? What has Jesus done for those who are free?

2. List the contrasts between those free and those not (John 8:31–59).

3. Did the Jews view themselves as slaves or free men? Why?

4. What are the elements of the gospel described in John 8:31–59?

5. What does Jesus say in response to the Jews in John 8:44?

6. Jesus claims to be *I AM*, our eternal Jehovah—a covenant keeping God (John 8:58). How did the Jews respond?

7. Have you been set free by the Son?

8. What truths can you claim from John 8:31–59?

Part Three: Two Sons, Two Covenants

1. What does Paul tell us about Abraham's sons (4:22)? Read Genesis 15:1–5 for the background information.

2. What did God promise Abram?

3. What other information is known of Abraham's faith? Cross-reference

Hebrews 11:8–10; Genesis 16:1–6, 15. How do you see God's grace shown in Abraham's life?

4. Had God forgotten his promise to aging Abraham? Read Genesis 17:1–21 and 21:1–7.

5. What does this tell us about God?

6. Could you wait patiently for this long?

7. What does Paul tell us about Abraham's two sons (4:22, 29)? How were the two sons alike? How were they different?

8. Paul writes that the two women are two covenants. What is a *covenant*? Review 3:15–18 in Lesson Eight, Part Three.

9. Complete the chart below using 4:22–31 to help you better understand what Scripture teaches about Hagar and Sarah.

Lesson Twelve 117

Hagar and the Covenant of Works	Sarah and the Covenant of Grace

10. Why does Paul point out that Abraham had another son by another woman?

11. How did Abraham and Sarah depend on their own efforts to help God with his promise? What had they forgotten?

12. Have you been guilty of trying to help God along or do you patiently wait for him to do the impossible?

Part Four: True Heirs

1. Why does Paul say these facts can be interpreted allegorically (4:24)?

2. Read Romans 9:4–18. What does this passage teach about God?

3. What does Romans 9:4–18 state about the Israelites?

4. How does Romans 9:4–18 further explain 4:22–31?

5. Who is a true *heir* (according to the Romans passage)? On what does your standing with God depend?

6. Hagar represents righteousness through the law and Sarah, righteousness by faith. What did Paul previously say in 2:16, 21?

7. How does Paul conclude Galatians 4?

8. Ultimately what does Paul want for the Galatians?

9. What do the Galatians want for themselves?

Part Five: Seeking Spiritual Freedom

1. What have you learned about the faithfulness of God? What have you learned about the sovereignty of God?

2. Consult commentaries to further extend your understanding of Galatians 4.

3. What does God want from you? Cross-reference Hebrews 11:6.

4. Do you more closely identify with Sarah or Hagar? Explain your answer.

5. If you know you are spiritually free because you have been justified by faith in Christ (2:16), take time to thank him. Ask for protection from the subtle lure of legalism. If you are seeking spiritual freedom, then there's good news for you! Jesus Christ died for sinners.

For Further Study
Ordo Salutis: The Order of Salvation

Adapted from a sermon preached by Dr. Michael F. Ross, Pastor Emeritus of Christ Covenant Church on July 17, 2011.

Latin: *ordo* (line, row, series, order, or the methodological arrangement); *salutis* (health, welfare, safety, or "salvation"). English: "the way of salvation."

Read Romans 8:28–30 and Titus 3:4–7.

Below is a brief but comprehensive understanding of how a person is saved. (The verses noted are by no means exhaustive.)

- Foreknowledge and predestination (Romans 8:29–30)
- Effectual calling (Romans 8:28–30)
- Regeneration (Titus 3:4–7)
- Conversion: repentance and faith (Ephesians 2:4–9)
- Justification (Romans 5:6–10, Titus 3:7)
- Adoption and assurance (Romans 8:15, Galatians 4:4–6, 1 John 5:13)
- Sanctification (1 Thessalonians 5:23–24, 2 Thessalonians 2:13–14)
- Perseverance (Philippians 1:6, Ephesians 1:13–14, Romans 8:37–39)
- Glorification in heaven (Romans 8:18, 2 Corinthians 2:14–18)

1. How do you see the Trinity at work in salvation? Use the references above to complete the following chart.

Work of God the Father	Work of Jesus, God the Son

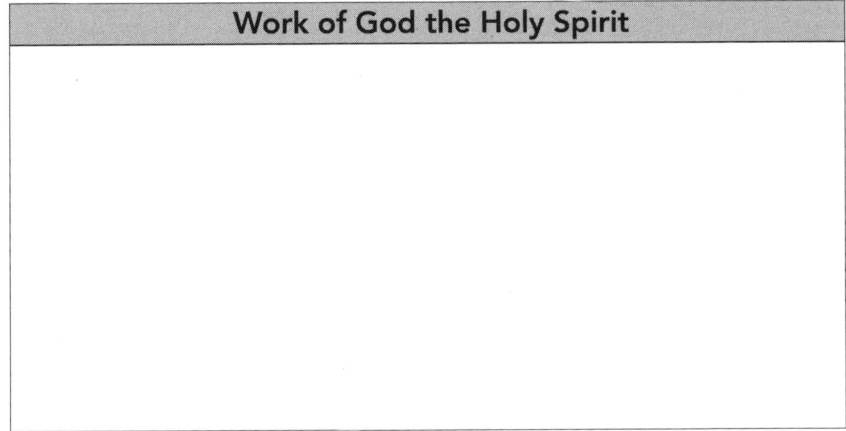

2. What did you do to gain or earn salvation? How does knowing that your salvation is based on God's sovereign and good pleasure affect how you think about God? Are you beginning to increase in your understanding of Paul's defense of the gospel in the book of Galatians?

Notes on Galatians Chapter 4

Gospel Freedom

Lesson Thirteen: Galatians 5:1–12

Part One: Chapter Survey

Prayerfully read Galatians chapter five.

1. What words or phrases are repeated in chapter five?

2. Read chapter five and mark in red every reference to God (Father, Jesus Christ, Holy Spirit). Fill in the chart with facts about God from this chapter.

Father	Son	Holy Spirit

3. Based on the facts in the chart above, describe God. Who is he?

4. What information does Paul tell us about himself? Note every time *Paul* is mentioned and color-code his name and any reference to his name (pronouns) in light blue. Note all that he wanted the Galatians to know about him.

5. Note every time the author mentions the recipients (*you* or *your*); color any reference to the recipients in orange. What do you learn about the Galatians?

6. What additional information is given about the false teachers?

7. List the questions Paul asked the Galatians in chapter five.

8. What is the main verse for chapter five? Give this chapter a title.

9. How does chapter four end and chapter five begin? Why are the Galatians free?

Part Two: Freedom in Christ

1. Read 5:1–2. What two exhortations did Paul give? Why?

2. What is a *yoke*? Take a few minutes to research this useful piece of equipment (use a study Bible or Bible dictionary).

3. Consider the context. What does Paul mean by a *yoke of slavery*?

4. Define *yoke 2218* and *of slavery 1397*. What was your former yoke of slavery? What is tempting you now to take up a yoke of slavery?

5. What is the opposite of a yoke of slavery? Define *freedom 1657*.

6. What do you learn about the word *freedom* in 2:4, 5:13; Acts 13:39; and 2 Corinthians 3:17?

7. Does freedom give one the right to live how she pleases?

8. How were the Galatians to live out their freedoms?

9. How are you to live out your freedoms?

10. Can one's freedom in Christ be lost?

Part Three: Stand Firm Therefore

1. What are the Galatians in danger of *again*? Read chapter five and note the consequences for submitting *again* to a yoke of slavery.

2. Is Paul against circumcision? Review circumcision (from Lesson Five,

Part Four) and then answer the following questions.

    a. Was circumcision bad?

    b. What did circumcision represent?

    c. Was circumcision a result of the law?

    d. Why was circumcision an issue that Paul had to deal with?

3. While we do not practice circumcision for salvation, what are some of the things we do or don't do to try to make ourselves *more* right with God? Is it possible to be more saved, more justified, more right with God? Read Romans 3:21–31.

4. What does Peter say about false teachers and their promises (2 Peter 2:19)? What had overcome the false teachers in Galatia?

5. Yet believers are to take a yoke. Read Matthew 11:28–30.

    a. Who is your Master? What is he like?

Lesson Thirteen

b. What are you to do with his yoke?

c. How does this encourage you?

d. Contrast the difference between the Master's yoke and the Judaizers' yoke.

6. Have you ever yoked yourself with guilt and condemnation?

7. What burdens might we carry as a result of not keeping the law perfectly? Cross-reference Romans 8:1–2. Define *condemnation 2631*. What did Christ free you from? How would this passage have been an encouragement to a Galatian?

8. What are we to do with our freedom (5:1)? Define *stand firm 4739*.

9. How do we stand firm? Cross-reference 1 Corinthians 16:13; Philippians 1:27–28, 4:1; and 1 Thessalonians 3:7–8.

10. How are you encouraged to stand firm in the freedom you have in Christ and not submit to a yoke of slavery?

Part Four: Jesus Broke the Power of the Devil

1. Read 5:1–4. Why was circumcision important to the false teachers?

2. What are the three ramifications of accepting circumcision (5:2–4)?

3. What does 5:4 teach? What does it not teach? How does Paul explain himself in 5:5–6?

4. Define *sever 2673* and *fallen away 1601*. Read from commentary resources for further clarification.

5. Were the Galatians desiring to *be justified* by the law (5:4)? (Review *jus-*

tification from Lesson Six, Parts Two-Three.) What were they attempting by their works?

6. Does circumcision or uncircumcision matter spiritually in the life of a believer? What are the evidences of salvation (5:5–6)? Cross-reference 1 John 2:2–6 and 19.

7. Write a modern version of 5:6, applying the truth that Paul emphasized. (For example, "For in Christ Jesus neither homeschooling nor public schooling counts for anything, but only faith working through love.")

8. Are you working for the hope of righteousness, or eagerly waiting for it? What effect does your certain future hope have on your life now?

9. What does Paul say about the false teachers in 5:7–12?

10. Ultimately, who is always at the root of hindering, persuading, deceiv-

ing, and bewitching the people of God? Cross-reference Hebrews 2:14–15, 1 John 3:8–10, Revelation 12:12.

Part Five: Purge the Evil from among You

1. Read 5:9–12. What was just a little bit of law doing to the churches in Galatia? What did Paul call it (5:9)?

2. What are possible consequences of the false teachers adding a little law (leaven)? Define *leaven 2219*.

3. Is Paul worried about the Galatians' perseverance in the faith (5:10–11)? What does he know to be true of the false teachers? Look back to 1:7–9.

4. Was there ever a time that Paul preached circumcision? Could Paul prove that he was only preaching salvation by faith?

5. What did Paul declare regarding the false teachers (5:12)? Define

emasculate 609. Read this verse in other translations to help you better understand Paul's sentiment.

6. How would Paul rate in the popularity polls of our culture today?

7. Is there ever a time when works saves a person? Can your works ever bribe God?

8. Read from commentary resources on 5:1–12 and summarize the passage.

9. Spend time in prayer asking the Lord for discernment that you would be able to detect error and stand firm. Thank Jesus for his grace.

For Further Study
Differences in Family

1. Read 4:1–5:1. Note the information appropriate to the columns below. Is Hagar or Sarah the mother of the true children of Abraham?

2. What are the differing characteristics of Hagar's and Sarah's sons? Review 2:16.

3. Read 3:2–27. Add additional facts from this passage in the chart.

Characteristics of a son born of Hagar	Characteristics of a son born of Sarah

4. Review the lists in each column. Why are we blessed to have Sarah as our mother?

5. What mothering qualities can we mimic from our mother, Sarah?

6. Praise God for freedom in Christ!

Covenant Community

Lesson Fourteen: Galatians 5:13–26

Part One: Perfect Love

1. What has Paul been reminding his readers? Prayerfully read Galatians chapters one through five for context. Reflect on previous lessons, thinking back on what you have learned, and recall what the Galatians had forgotten.

2. What were the Galatians called to (5:13)? What were they called from (1:4)? Describe this incredible transfer from darkness to light.

3. What is Paul warning the Galatians in 5:13? What is the better alternative?

4. The Galatians had been set free. How might they have used their freedom for an opportunity for the flesh?

5. How were the Galatians to serve one another? Read 5:13–26. Mark the word *love* with a red heart. Note what you learn about *love* in this section.

6. What one word fulfills the whole law (5:14)? What kind of love does Paul have in mind for the Spirit-filled life? Cross-reference Matthew 22:36–40, Leviticus 19:18, and Deuteronomy 6:5.

7. How were the Galatians able to love the way God intended? What do the following verses teach about God's love?

　a. Romans 5:5–8

　b. Romans 13:8–10

　c. Galatians 2:20